HELP!
I WANT TO CHANGE

Jim Newheiser

Consulting Editor: Dr. Paul Tautges

Help! I Want to Change

© 2014 by Jim Newheiser

ISBN
Paper: 978-1-63342-015-1
ePub: 978-1-63342-016-8
Kindle: 978-1-63342-01-5

Published by **Shepherd Press**
P.O. Box 24
Wapwallopen, PA 18660

www.shepherdpress.com

All Scripture quotations, unless stated otherwise, are
from the New American Standard Bible (NASB) Copyright
©1960, 1962, 1963, 1968, 1971, 1972, 1973, 1975, 1977,
1995 by The Lockman Foundation.

First printed by Day One Publications

Designed by **documen**

ENDORSEMENTS

Dr. Jim Newheiser explains, clearly and concisely, what God's Word teaches about the dynamics that enable deep transformation of our desires and behavior. He shows how God's grace in Christ ignites our response of love for God, and how the Spirit of God uses the gospel itself to motivate and empower us to resist habits and appetites that breed shame and defeat. He also demonstrates from the Scriptures the complementary truth that we need in our struggle against sin: that the grand indicatives of what Jesus has done for us and the assurance of the Father's invincible love toward us are intended not to make us passive, but to sustain our hope and to fire our resolve to fight sin and pursue Christlike holiness and love.

Dennis E. Johnson,
Professor, Practical Theology,
Westminster Seminary, California, USA

It's easy to see areas that need changing in our lives and, as Christians, we long for change that will glorify God. But how is change accomplished? In this helpful booklet, Jim Newheiser reminds us that change begins and is sustained by the power of Christ through the gospel, and that through that same gospel we are enabled to respond. I highly recommend it!

Elyse Fitzpatrick,
author, speaker, and counselor

In this little gem, Dr. Newheiser hits the nail squarely on the head! Read it and use it with confidence in Christ.

George C. Scipione,
Director, Biblical Counseling Institute,
Reformed Presbyterian Theological Seminary,
Pittsburgh, PA, USA

A byproduct of years of careful thinking by a bright-minded and caring counselor, this little booklet is densely packed with biblical guidance for any who are interested in transformation for themselves and others. I rejoice in the attention that this booklet gives to God as the Author of change and to the role played by gospel indicatives and imperatives in nurturing and directing the process of change. Readers will find much hope and help here!

Milton Vincent, author,
A Gospel Primer for Christians

CONTENTS

INTRODUCTION

We all have areas in our lives which we want to change. Some would like to have more discipline in their eating and exercise. Many know they need to establish budgets by which they can get their spending and credit card debts under control. Others wish they were more faithful in their daily Bible reading and prayer. But change is hard. Many have tried to change but have experienced a continuing cycle of failure.

Dan,[1] a young man in his early twenties, has been fighting the temptation of pornography and self-gratification ever since he became a Christian when he was in his mid-teens. He sometimes goes days or even weeks without giving in to lust. When he fails he confesses his sin to God, but the feelings of defeat and hopelessness linger for days.

Sally, a middle-aged stay-at-home wife, started drinking when her kids grew up and left home.

She has gone through various programs, but has never been able to go more than a month without going on a binge. She agreed to carry no cash or credit cards so that she wouldn't possess the means to buy alcohol, but one day recently she was so desperate that she pawned silver which has been in the family for generations to get the money to indulge her habit.

Jim has struggled with his weight all his life. As he has grown older and heavier his doctor has put him on cholesterol medication and is about to put him on blood pressure drugs. Jim knows exactly what he should do—eat less and exercise more. In the last six years he has started diet and fitness programs countless times, but he never sticks with them for more than a few days.

Bob and Mary have been married for over ten years. The Lord has blessed them with a son, aged eight, and a daughter, five. Bob and Mary don't fight, but there is no intimacy in their relationship. They also recognize that they aren't being wise and consistent in raising their children. They are both tired of the mediocrity of their family life, but they feel powerless to make things better.

Vic has an explosive temper which has cost him relationships with friends and family members, and in his career. He has been to anger management classes, once by court order after an incident in which the police were called out because he had physically assaulted his younger brother. When Vic is calm he knows the right things to say and do, but when he is provoked everything he has learned goes out the window and he blows up.

Dan, Sally, Jim, Bob, Mary, and Vic all want to know *"Why can't we change?"*

The Bible teaches principles by which we can experience significant changes in our lives. The change that we, as biblical Christians, seek is unique. Our goal is not merely to transform some aspect of our lives so that we will be happier or more comfortable. The goal of believers is that we would become more Christlike and that this change would be to the glory of God (Colossians 1:28; 1 Timothy 4:5; 1 Corinthians 10:31). God desires this kind of change in his people and is committed to seeing that it happens:

> I am confident of this very thing, that
> He who began a good work in you will
> perfect it until the day of Christ Jesus.
> (Philippians 1:6)

This is good news!

1

Unbiblical Methods
Lead to Failure

Many professing Christians seek change in their lives using methods which are contrary to Scripture. As a result, they don't experience the change which God seeks to produce in his people. Consider just six examples.

Deliverance Ministries

Some claim that the source of every personal problem is demonic and that the solution is to identify and cast out the evil spirit(s). Certain preachers claim to have the special powers and methods to perform these deliverances. They often draw large crowds of people desperate for help. While the Bible does teach that we are engaged in spiritual warfare (Ephesians 6:11–12), it does not teach that all our spiritual problems can be solved by casting out demons. If this were the issue, the Bible would contain detailed instructions for how to identify and eliminate demons. Those who seek such unbiblical deliverances typically fall into their old patterns again and again. Instead, we are taught to engage in spiritual warfare by putting on the armor of God, which includes truth, righteousness, the gospel, faith, salvation, Scripture, and prayer (Ephesians 6:13–18).

Mysticism

Many believers expect that God will somehow instantly zap away their sin patterns and problems through dramatic answers to certain kinds of prayers. Some seek out spiritual leaders who claim to have special powers in prayer to produce dramatic results. The Bible, on the other hand, teaches that spiritual growth and true wisdom are typically obtained through a persistent disciplined pursuit of God (Proverbs 2:2–12), not through a one-time experience. Many repeatedly go through such emotional experiences, only to have the sin pattern resume after the excitement and feelings wear off. They are then tempted to be angry with God, blaming him for not taking away the sin. Others passively continue in their sin, excusing themselves by the claim that they cannot change until God mystically intervenes.

Medication

While we embrace the use of medicine for true medical problems, many believers are hoping to find quick and easy solutions to their spiritual problems through pills. Some drugs may dull some of the symptoms of our emotional pain, but they do not address the heart issues from which sin comes (Proverbs 4:23; Mark 7:20–23).[2]

Self-Improvement Formulas

Worldly methods of change typically involve finding the resources within yourself to successfully lose weight, stop smoking, control anger, and so on. This is contrary to Scripture, which teaches that we are totally dependent upon God for meaningful transformation. Jesus said,

> Apart from Me you can do nothing.
>
> (John 15:5)

Moralism

Many try to change by seeking to discipline themselves to do the "right thing" by keeping a list of rules. God's Word teaches that we can't keep

God's law in our own power (Romans 3:20) and that we cannot be truly changed merely by keeping rules.

> For what the Law could not do, weak as it
> was through the flesh, God did: sending
> His own Son ...
>
> (Romans 8:3)

Those pursuing moralistic solutions will either have to lower their standards far below those of Scripture, resulting in pride, or they will endure an endless cycle of failure, resulting in despair.

Recovery Programs

Twelve-step programs, such as Alcoholics Anonymous, are very widely used by those who seek to make significant changes in their lives. Such programs typically combine elements of mysticism (relying on an undefined higher power), self-improvement formulas, and moralism, while neglecting the biblical instructions as to how we can change.

In contrast to all these methods, Scripture teaches us that God transforms us as we understand and experience the power of the gospel and then step forward in Spirit-enabled obedience.

2
The Gospel Is the Key to Change

Many Christians think that the gospel is important only at the beginning of the Christian life. They understand it merely as the means by which our sins are forgiven by faith in Christ (justification), failing to see the importance of the gospel for our ongoing growth as Christians (sanctification). Many believe that while we are justified (declared righteous by God) through grace, we are then sanctified (changed and made more holy) primarily by law. This, however, is not the pattern exhibited in the Scriptures. Paul admonishes the Galatians,

> Are you so foolish? Having begun by the Spirit, are you now being perfected by the flesh?
>
> (Galatians 3:3)

Christians still need the gospel—every day! Paul wrote to the believers in Rome that he earnestly desired to preach the gospel to them (Romans 1:15). He then spent several chapters giving the most magnificent explanation of the gospel contained in Scripture. Why did Paul think that these Roman Christians needed so much gospel?

Remember What God Has Done for You

Many of us, when trying to change (or to help others to change), rush to the commands of Scripture (what we should do for God) before having placed adequate emphasis upon what God has done for us (the gospel). We should learn from the typical pattern in the New Testament epistles, which is to begin with gospel truth (Romans 1–11; Ephesians 1–3; Colossians 1–2) before making practical application as to our duties (Romans 12–16; Ephesians 4–6; Colossians 3–4). The practical commands are based upon the preceding truth of God's wonderful gospel grace both in general (Romans 12:1; Ephesians 4:1) and in particular. Paul's well-known sequence of "put off"s and put-on's" is explicitly grounded in the gospel truth of who we are in Christ (Ephesians 4:20–24). We are to forgive because we have been forgiven through the gospel (Ephesians 4:32). We are to walk in love, just as God loved us and gave Christ for us as an offering and sacrifice (Ephesians 5:1–2). Husbands are to love their wives as Christ has loved the church (Ephesians 5:25–33).

The fact that the gospel comes first implies that only gospel-believing Christians are able to change in a way that glorifies God.

> The mind set on the flesh is hostile
> toward God; for it does not subject itself
> to the law of God, for it is not even able
> to do so, and those who are in the flesh
> cannot please God.
>
> (Romans 8:7–8)

Some might object; what about unbelievers who successfully quit drinking, stop smoking, or lose weight (for example, on the TV program *The Biggest Loser*)? It is true that non-Christians are capable of exercising self-discipline to obtain their goals in life. The difference is in motive. The only change that pleases God takes place by faith, through his power and for his glory (Hebrews 11:6; Romans 14:23; 1 Corinthians 10:31). When an unbeliever improves some aspect of his or her life (e.g. losing weight) it is for an inferior motive (e.g. so that he or she can feel better or will be more attractive to members of the opposite sex). A person may exchange the idol of food for the idols of sex and the approval of men and women, but he or she is still under the dominion of sin (see Matthew 12:43–45). The change that pleases God takes place when our hearts are changed by the power of the gospel and we are empowered not only to do what is right, but to do so for his glory.

Perhaps the reason you have been unable to change is that you have not yet experienced God's gracious love in Christ. Have you personally confessed your sin to God and called upon him to save you for Jesus' sake?

> Believe in the Lord Jesus, and you will be saved.
>
> (Acts 16:31)

Once you believe, God will work by his Holy Spirit in your life to make you more like Christ.

Your Standing with God Is Secure in Christ

Many believers, though they realize that they are justified by faith, still think that God accepts them according to how well they measure up to his standards (law). The young wife and mother believes that God is pleased when her home is in order, her children are well disciplined and her husband is pleased with her. But when her home is a mess, her children are rowdy, and the laundry isn't done, she then has the uneasy sense that God is upset with her. The young man who struggles with lust tends to think that when he has kept away from pornography and self-gratification he enjoys God's favor, but when he stumbles into sin he has lost his standing with God. The person who struggles with obesity is tempted to think that he or she is acceptable and worthy according to how thin he or she is.

However, the gospel declares that God accepts us for Christ's sake and that the only righteousness we possess is the perfect righteousness of Christ. Paul writes,

> I count all things to be loss in view of
> the surpassing value of knowing Christ
> Jesus my Lord, for whom I have suffered
> the loss of all things, and count them
> but rubbish so that I may gain Christ,
> and may be found in Him, not having a
> righteousness of my own derived from
> the Law, but that which is through faith
> in Christ, the righteousness which comes
> from God on the basis of faith.
>
> (Philippians 3:8–9)

God's regard for the Christian is based upon the perfect work of Jesus Christ. The homemaker is equally accepted whether her house is clean and dinner is on time or the house is a mess and dinner is late. The young man who struggles with lust has a perfect standing with God whether or not he has stumbled this week, because he is in Christ. The person who struggles with obesity is a beloved child of God, regardless of what he or she weighs. As a friend of mine put it, for the believer there are no merit meters which we must feed with merit tokens. We rest in the truth that we will never be more or less acceptable to God than we were on the day of our conversion.

The Gospel Promotes Holiness

Some might complain that such teaching of free grace will encourage people to continue sinning and to make no effort toward holiness.[3] Paul actually anticipated such an objection.

> What shall we say then? Are we to
> continue in sin so that grace may
> increase? May it never be! How shall we
> who died to sin still live in it?
> (Romans 6:1–2)

Paul states that the gospel, rightly understood, promotes holiness, not sin. He describes our union with Christ through the picture of baptism. When God saved you, your old self died with Jesus; you are now raised with him into a new life (Romans 6:3–5). John Stott described the experience of a believer as a two-volume biography.[4] Volume 1 is the life of the natural man, which begins with physical birth and ends when the old man died with Christ at the time of conversion. Just as the risen Jesus, having carried the penalty of our sin, was forever freed from sin's curse, so the believer is done with sin's bondage (Romans 6:8–10). Volume 2 begins with the new birth, which gives a person an entirely new nature. Just as Jesus was raised from the dead, never to die again, so you have been given new life with him (Romans 6:4–5).

Paul also describes conversion as being set free from slavery to sin and becoming a slave to God's righteousness (Romans 6:6–7, 9, 15–22). These realities are true of every believer, whether young or old, whether a new convert or a seasoned saint, whether she has had a good week or a bad week in her area of struggle, and whether he feels it or not. This is life-transforming truth!

Remember Who You Are

When I preached through the book of Romans I was surprised to find that the first command (imperative) in this great book does not occur until 6:11:

> Even so consider yourselves to be dead to sin, but alive to God in Christ Jesus.

Paul's first imperative was not that they stop sinning or start serving God (though these commands would come later). Rather, it was that they think correctly and intently about who they were in Christ. Remembering who we are in Christ is the key to change—overcoming sin and doing what is right.

A story is told of a young prince who, as he was leaving for school each day, was told by his mother, "Remember who you are!" She was concerned that he live up to his royal status. Paul is saying the same thing to the Christian believer: "Remember who you are in Christ!" He realizes that recalling that our old sinful nature has died with Christ and that we have a new, risen nature which is no longer enslaved to sin will motivate and empower us to change (live holy lives).

Sometimes it can be a challenge to live in light of who we are. The fact that we are united to Christ does not mean that it is no longer possible for us to sin. After the American Civil War, slavery was abolished; yet some former slaves had difficulty grasping their new status. When their old masters beckoned them to come back and serve them, some did, in spite of their position as free men and women.[5] In the same way, our old sinful nature tries to entice us to return to serving the flesh. When this happens we need to remember our new status as those who have been set free from sin and are now empowered to serve God.

Marriage provides another analogy. Is it possible for a married man to live as if he is single? In one sense he can, but he should not. His single life has ended and his new, married life has begun. He should look at his wedding ring (as Paul, in Romans 6, reminded us to look at our baptism), remember his status—"I am a married man"—and then live accordingly.

Before his conversion Pedro had been involved in drugs, theft, and violence through a gang. When God saved him Pedro sought to settle down in a new life with a legitimate job and a family. God has blessed Pedro with a wife and young daughter. Sadly, when Pedro and his wife have a conflict, he often reverts to his angry past. He says extremely hurtful things and has become physical, to the point that his wife has threatened to call the police. After their fights Pedro, in anger and shame, often leaves the house and hangs out on the streets, where he meets up with his old friends, does drugs, and gets into fights. After a few days, he returns home with a broken heart, and he and his wife are reconciled.

The damage from these episodes is mounting. Pedro knows this pattern must be changed. He realizes that he needs to control his temper and that it is wrong to do drugs, but he keeps failing. What can he do? I took Pedro through Romans 6 and reminded him of his union with Christ. I encouraged him to memorize Romans 6:3–6; Romans 6:11; and Ephesians 4:32. When Pedro finds himself in situations in which he feels tempted to become angry he needs to tell himself, "I am no longer the man I used to be. The angry, abusive Pedro died with Christ. I am now raised with Christ and am no longer enslaved to sin. As God has shown great mercy to me, so I can be patient and merciful with others."

A Liberating Truth!

Many Christians have a false identity in which they are labeled according to their past slavery to sin rather than according to their new identity in Christ. For example, some are labeled addicts or abusers and are told that that is who they are and always will be. This is contrary to Paul's teaching in Romans 6, that we have a new nature in union with Christ, and in 2 Corinthians 5:17, where he says,

> Therefore if anyone is in Christ, he is a
> new creature; the old things passed away;
> behold, new things have come.

I once counseled a man who was very discouraged because he had been told that he was an alcoholic and that would be his identity for life. I got him to read 1 Corinthians 6:9–11, which states,

> Or do you not know that the unrighteous
> will not inherit the kingdom of God? Do
> not be deceived; neither fornicators, nor
> idolaters, nor adulterers, nor effeminate,
> nor homosexuals, nor thieves, nor the
> covetous, nor drunkards, nor revilers,

> nor swindlers, will inherit the kingdom
> of God. Such were some of you; but you
> were washed, but you were sanctified, but
> you were justified in the name of the Lord
> Jesus Christ and in the Spirit of our God.

I focused my friend's attention on the second word in verse 11. After Paul listed all those heinous sins, he didn't say "such *are* you," but "such *were* you"—past tense. I told my friend, "Because you are in Christ, the gospel has changed your identity forever. You are no longer to think of yourself as what you were, but rather as what you are in Christ: a cleansed sinner." The former drunkard wept with joy.

This is also true for every other kind of sinner. The gospel not only forgives homosexuals, gluttons, and thieves, it also transforms them into new people whose lives are no longer characterized and identified by these sins. This is good news!

Christ is Better Than the Sins Which Tempt Us

People turn to sin—whether it be gluttony, substance abuse, lust, or materialism—seeking some kind of satisfaction. But the Lord calls out to us in Isaiah 55:1–2,

Ho! Everyone who thirsts, come to the
waters;
And you who have no money come, buy
and eat.
Come, buy wine and milk
Without money and without cost.
Why do you spend money for what is not
bread,
And your wages for what does not satisfy?
Listen carefully to Me, and eat what is
good,
And delight yourself in abundance.

The bad habits (substance abuse, overspending, immorality, etc.) to which we keep turning for fulfillment don't satisfy us. They just make us miserable and ashamed. When we seek satisfaction in these instead of in God, we make them into idols. God offers something so much better. To illustrate: If a toddler is playing with a sharp knife, one way to deliver him or her from danger is to grab the knife. Another, perhaps more effective, method would be to offer the child a piece of candy, for which he or she will gladly let go of the knife. This is how God motivates us to let go of our favorite (dangerous) sins. God does not merely take away our sin idols. He offers us something much better in their place. Jesus uses the same kind of language speaking of himself:

> He who believes in Me, as the Scripture said, "From his innermost being will flow rivers of living water."
>
> (John 7:38)

> I am the bread of life; he who comes to Me will not hunger, and he who believes in Me will never thirst.
>
> (John 6:35)

> Your fathers ate the manna in the wilderness, and they died. This is the bread which comes down out of heaven, so that one may eat of it and not die. I am the living bread that came down out of heaven; if anyone eats of this bread, he will live forever; and the bread also which I will give for the life of the world is My flesh.
>
> (John 6:49–51)

A key to overcoming any temptation (experiencing change) is realizing that Christ is more satisfying, more enjoyable, than the misuse of food, alcohol, sex, or material things. When tempted, we need to learn to "Taste and see that the LORD is good" (Psalm 34:8), as we learn to feed by faith on Christ instead of trying to satisfy ourselves in the broken cisterns of the world. The lonely, discouraged glutton who is tempted to eat some candy as a kind of drug to make her feel better can instead choose to turn to Christ and be filled spiritually. The man who is tempted to go into debt to buy a new electronic gadget can forsake the temporary "buzz" his new toy offers so that he might have more of Christ, in whom there is unmixed joy and satisfaction.

Martha has been struggling with depression. She is in a hard marriage and her problems are compounded by the fact that two of her children have special needs and require much extra attention. Martha has been leaving her husband at home with the kids at night and going back to the party and drinking scene which was a part of her life before she became a Christian. She says that she needs her nights out to relieve her stress after a hard day of caring for her kids. How can Martha be helped? Just telling her to stop may not convince her to give up the earthly pleasures for which she has been living. Martha needs to see that she is vainly seeking satisfaction from earthly idols which will never fulfill her, and that only Christ can satisfy the needs of her soul. Drawing near to him by faith will produce in her a joy and a peace which the world cannot give.

Christ Empowers Us to Bear Fruit

Jesus declares in John 15:5,

> I am the vine, you are the branches; he who abides in Me and I in him, he bears much fruit, for apart from Me you can do nothing.

Just as the branch cannot bear fruit without being connected to the vine, so we cannot bear spiritual fruit (see Galatians 5:22–23) of lives transformed for God's glory unless we abide in Christ. The believer who tries to change by his or her own power will fail. This may be why you have been unable to get your eating, drinking, or spending under control.

How, then, does one abide in Christ? The answer is contained in the surrounding verses: by filling your mind with his Word:

> If you abide in Me, and My words abide in

you, ask whatever you wish, and it will be
done for you.

(John 15:7)

This verse also teaches that we abide in Christ
through dependent prayer, asking him to work
in us what we are completely unable to do on
our own. Jesus also links our abiding in him to
obedience to his commandments:

If you keep My commandments, you will
abide in My love.

(John 15:10a)

Obedience to the commandment to love one
another is a particularly important aspect of
abiding in Christ (John 15:12–13). Elsewhere
John writes,

The one who says he abides in Him ought
himself to walk in the same manner as
He walked.

(1 John 2:6)

When Dan experiences failure in his struggle
against lust, rather than wallowing in defeat
or merely purposing to fight harder in his own

strength, he turns to Christ. He is thankful that even though he has sinned, God graciously invites him to return:

> Seek the LORD while He may be found;
> Call upon Him while He is near.
> Let the wicked forsake his way
> And the unrighteous man his thoughts;
> And let him return to the LORD,
> And He will have compassion on him,
> And to our God,
> For He will abundantly pardon.
>
> (Isaiah 55:6–7)

Dan doesn't merely confess his sin of lust, but more importantly he acknowledges that he failed because he wasn't consciously and dependently abiding in Christ. As Dan draws near to the Lord through the Word and prayer he is transformed from a dry, dead branch into a man bearing fruit to the glory of God.

Summary: Change Begins with the Gospel

As we remember what God has done for us in setting us free from sin and giving us a new identity in union with Christ, we are transformed inwardly. As we learn to satisfy our souls with the spiritual feast God has given us in Christ, we abide in him and bear much fruit. As our hearts are continually filled with thoughts of God's love and grace toward us, we are able to show love and grace to others.

We love, because He first loved us.

(1 John 4:19)

The kindness of God leads you to repentance.

(Romans 2:4b)

3

Your Responsibility toward Change

We have already seen that the gospel (what God has done for us) is the key to change and that what we do for God is secondary, in response to his grace. Some, perhaps reacting against their legalistic past, focus solely upon God's work for us and are extremely reluctant to exhort people to exert obedient effort toward change. They may even accuse those who counsel or preach obedience to God's law of being moralistic. I once counseled a husband and wife who had gone to a pastor seeking help with the husband's addiction to pornography. Their pastor's counsel was simply "Look to Christ." The wife asked, "Isn't there something concrete we should do? Should we put a block or filter on our computer? Could a man in the church meet with my husband weekly for accountability?" The pastor said, "I can't tell you to do any of those things. All I can tell you to do is look to Christ."

Getting the Balance Right

If you have carefully read the preceding chapter, you will know that I completely agree that looking to Christ (focusing upon the transforming power of the gospel) is the key to spiritual growth (change). We have seen that the New Testament epistles typically begin with the indicative, what God has done for us. But the New Testament authors also proclaim the imperative which follows from the indicative. There are practical principles in the New Testament which could help the person who is struggling with lust:

> *Flee from youthful lusts.*
>
> *(2 Timothy 2:22)*

> *If your right eye makes you stumble,*
> *tear it out and throw it from you; for it is*
> *better for you to lose one of the parts of*
> *your body, than for your whole body to be*
> *thrown into hell.*
>
> *(Matthew 5:29)*

So, for example, it would be better to live without the Internet than to continually fall into sin while using the Internet.

One woman said, "I come to church, not to hear about what I must do for God, but to hear about what God has done for me." I can appreciate her concern that what God has done for us in the gospel is the most important aspect of worship (and counseling). Perhaps she had bad experiences in churches which have wrongly assumed that the gospel is primarily for unbelievers, and therefore their ministry to Christians focused almost exclusively upon moral duty, without continually pointing them back to Christ. Perhaps she has experienced years of defeat in her own Christian walk by pounding herself with God's law. Now that she has understood the freeing power of the gospel, she becomes disturbed by any call to obedience. Or perhaps her former church was faithfully preaching the gospel, but her own past tendency to legalism caused her to focus on the imperative (our duty) and to take the indicative (what God has done for us in Christ) for granted. This sister has, however, created a harmful false dichotomy between proclaiming the gospel and our obedient response to the gospel. The Scriptures contain the perfect order and balance which begins with what God has done for us as the basis for our gospel obedience.

John Murray writes,

> *The pilgrimage to perfection (in the*
> *eternal state) is not one of quiescence*
> *and inactivity. It is not "let go and let*
> *God." The journey proceeds apace with*
> *the most intense exercise on our part ...*
> *Our working is not suspended because*
> *God works, and God's working is not*
> *suspended because we work ... They*
> *are complementary ... Our working is*
> *grounded in God's working. Our working*
> *receives its urge, strength, incentive, and*
> *cause from God's working in us.*[6]

As we seek to minister the biblical truths
concerning both God's work in the gospel and our
obedience, different people may require different
emphases. Paul writes,

> We urge you, brethren, admonish the
> unruly, encourage the fainthearted, help
> the weak, be patient with everyone.
>   (1 Thessalonians 5:14)

Those who have had legalistic tendencies and
have been beating themselves up over their many
sinful failures, in spite of their best efforts to obey
God, may be the fainthearted or the weak who

need to be encouraged and helped. They should be reminded that their perfection and virtue are found only in Christ, not in their performance. They are fully accepted by God because the righteousness of Christ has been given to them as a gift (Philippians 3:9). On the other hand, some professing Christians make little or no effort toward obedience. I knew a man who was a very poor husband and father. His attitude was, "Because salvation is all God's work, it is not my job to try harder. Instead, I will wait for God to change me." Such a man appears to be unruly and needs to be admonished. John writes,

> By this we know that we have
> come to know Him, if we keep His
> commandments. The one who says, "I
> have come to know Him," and does not
> keep His commandments, is a liar, and
> the truth is not in him.
>
> (1 John 2:3–4)

Jesus said,

> If you love Me, you will keep My
> commandments.
>
> (John 14:15)

He also warned,

> You will know them by their fruits.
> (Matthew 7:20)

What Is the Purpose of God's Law?

The law has a vital role in bringing unbelievers to conversion. Paul states in Galatians 3:24,

> Therefore the Law has become our tutor
> to lead us to Christ, so that we may be
> justified by faith.

Unsaved people typically think that they are good because they can follow a standard of human morality. When the unbeliever sees the true heart-meaning of God's law, he or she is driven by the inability to keep God's commandments to see his or her need of Christ's atonement and righteousness, which come as God's gift through faith. What some don't adequately appreciate is that God's law continues to play this kind of role in the life of believers. Our daily failure to perfectly keep God's commandments drives us back to the comfort of the gospel, which reminds us that our standing before God comes solely through faith in

Christ and not by our works. Our sin drives us to recognize our daily need for the gospel of grace.

God's commandments have an additional function for a Christian. God's law shows us how he desires his redeemed people to live. Because we love God, who so graciously saved us, we are eager to please him by living the holy, fruitful lives which are produced by the work of the gospel within us. Paul, speaking of Christ, says he

> gave Himself for us to redeem us from
> every lawless deed, and to purify for
> Himself a people for His own possession,
> zealous for good deeds.
>
> (Titus 2:14)

Christ died, not merely that we might be forgiven, but also that we might be holy. We should pursue holiness with passion, seeking to do the good deeds in which our Lord delights. We, like the recipients of the New Testament epistles, often need to be admonished to that end.

Elyse Fitzpatrick and Dennis Johnson write of how the grace of God in the gospel empowers and motivates our obedience:

> *Since we cannot be made any more perfect*

in God's eyes than we already are, we are
now free to make the law serve us. It will
serve us by making us more thankful for
Christ when we see how we fail to obey it,
and it will serve us by showing us how to
love God and our neighbor as we long to.
Rather than viewing the law as our enemy,
we'll learn to say along with our Savior,
"I delight to do your will, O my God; Your
law is within my heart" (Psalm 40:8).[7]

Scriptural Examples of the Call to Gospel Obedience

Immediately after commanding us to consider our identity as being dead to sin and alive to God in Christ (Romans 6:11), Paul exhorts us,

> Therefore do not let sin reign in your
> mortal body so that you obey its lusts,
> and do not go on presenting the members
> of your body to sin as instruments of
> unrighteousness; but present yourselves
> to God as those alive from the dead,
> and your members as instruments of
> righteousness to God.
>
> (Romans 6:12–13)

Your old nature is trying to regain control of you by means of your fleshly appetites. Don't yield an inch.

As mentioned earlier, the typical pattern in the New Testament epistles is to first declare God's work through Christ (e.g. Ephesians 1–3; Colossians 1–2; Romans 1–11), but then to call readers to live in light of this gospel (Ephesians 4–6; Colossians 3–4; Romans 12–16). After his magnificent unfolding of God's glorious plan of salvation in Romans 1–11, Paul writes,

> Therefore I urge you, brethren, by the
> mercies of God, to present your bodies
> a living and holy sacrifice, acceptable to
> God, which is your spiritual service of
> worship. And do not be conformed to
> this world, but be transformed by the
> renewing of your mind, so that you may
> prove what the will of God is, that which
> is good and acceptable and perfect.
>
> (Romans 12:1–2)

Those who have embraced these wondrous truths of God's mercy will want to give their lives to God. They will gladly turn their back on the world so that they might serve our gracious

Lord. Paul goes on to exhort the Romans on many specific issues, including their duties to love and serve one another, to respect civil authorities, and to be willing to defer on matters of conscience. The same pattern can be observed throughout most of the other New Testament epistles which typically start with the gospel but go on to give us necessary practical instruction for every aspect of life, including our speech, how we conduct ourselves in our families, how to live under persecution, how to resolve conflict, and so on.[8]

Jesus also emphasized the importance of obedience, warning that those who hear his Word without acting upon it are like a man who builds his house on the sand and whose fall will be great when the storm comes; those who act upon his words are like a wise man who builds his life on the stable rock, which can withstand the floods (Matthew 7:24–27). His call to discipleship is a call to radical obedience.

> If anyone wishes to come after Me, he
> must deny himself, and take up his cross
> and follow Me.
>
> (Mark 8:34b)

If simply proclaiming and meditating upon the

gospel would produce biblical change, the New Testament authors would not have been guided by the Holy Spirit to exhort believers to actively resist temptation to sin and to strive after good works of obedience. While the greatest need of believers is to more fully know the gospel, we also need to hear and heed God's commands. It is not enough to merely listen to the gospel—we need to act upon it (James 1:22).

Our Motive for Obedience Is Crucial

Most religions teach that we should do what is morally right so that we might earn God's favor. Christianity is unique when it teaches that we can never be justified before God by our works (Romans 3:20) and that we are saved by God's grace alone (Ephesians 2:8–9). We already enjoy God's complete favor because he has given us the perfect righteousness of Christ as a gift through faith (Philippians 3:9). Our good works of obedience and service can't add to the merit of Christ which has been imputed to us. Nor do we do what is good and right so that we can feel better about ourselves. The best of us is still the chief of sinners (1 Timothy 1:15). We obey, not to gain God's favor, but out of love for and gratitude to him who so loved us when we deserved only wrath.

A few years ago, as Valentine's Day was approaching, my wife came to me and said, "Jim, I love you, and I know that you love me, so you don't have to buy me anything this year for Valentine's Day." Now I realize that from some women such words might be insincere, and that the husband had better come up with an exceptional gift or else he would be in the doghouse! But as I thought about what Caroline had said, I realized that she meant it. If I gave her nothing at all for Valentine's Day she would love me just as much and treat me just as well as if I had given her the most amazing gift. I also realized that if I were to buy her a nice gift, it wouldn't gain me any more favor than I already have. I am already as loved and accepted as I can be. What do you think that I did as a result? Did I say to myself, "Great! I don't have to buy her a gift, so I have more time and money to spend on myself"? No! Instead, my heart was moved by such love that I wanted to respond by loving her in return. As I thought further about this, I realized that this kind of experience in marriage illustrates how God's love in the gospel moves us to obedience and change. Our works of obedience do not add to the righteousness of Christ which has already been imputed to us. Nor can our service make him love us more. God is already as favorably disposed toward us as he can possibly be. We love (and obey) God, not in order to cause him to love us, or to make him love us more than he already does, but because he first loved us (1 John 4:19).

4
When Will Change Take Place?

During the past twenty years of working in a church-based biblical counseling ministry, in which I have tried to put these principles for change into practice, I have observed three general outcomes. Some counselees are quickly and radically transformed. I have seen cases in which a husband and wife who were already separated and moving toward divorce were in one session brought to heartbroken repentance as each confessed his or her own sin (Matthew 7:1–5) and granted forgiveness to the other, in light of the forgiveness we have received in the gospel (Ephesians 4:32; Matthew 18:21–35). I have also seen many cases in which the counselees went away sad and unchanged, like the rich young ruler (Mark 10:17–22). There are also cases in which change takes place gradually, at an almost glacial pace. We seek to give the same biblical, gospel-centered counsel to everyone who comes, but the results vary widely. Why is this?

We have also had experiences when we have labored over situations for months, with little progress, only to have the counselees come back, perhaps years later, having been radically changed after attending a conference, reading a book, or speaking to someone else. It can be maddening, because what they finally learned is what we had been repeatedly telling them. Why did it finally work when other people said the same thing?

I can also look back on my own personal experience, remembering some sins which were quickly put away. For example, immediately after I was converted I no longer had a desire to use foul language. On the other hand, I have had to wage extended battles against other sins, such as the temptation to use food as a comfort and thereby overeat (gluttony). There have been periodic struggles, such as an extended season of depression I endured when adult sons turned away from the faith and which gradually lifted after a few very hard years. While I am thankful that God kept me from falling during those hard years, I don't fully understand his timing in bringing me back to my normal driven self.

God Is the Author of Change

Sometimes change doesn't take place because a person is not truly saved. Jesus speaks of people who claim to belong to him, but whose fruit proves otherwise. He says that he never knew them, meaning that they were never truly converted (Matthew 7:15–23). Jesus also warns that fruitless branches, which symbolize people who falsely claim a connection with him, will be cut off (John 15:2, 6). James warns that those who say that they have faith but don't have any works do not have true saving faith (James 2:14–26). Paul states in Philippians 1:6,

> For I am confident of this very thing, that
> He who began a good work in you will
> perfect it until the day of Christ Jesus.

If God has begun the work in someone through renewing and justifying him or her, God will continue the work by continuing to grow that person in holiness. If there is no spiritual change, it is because the work has not yet begun. The commands of Scripture call converted people to act according to the new nature God has given them. Unbelievers are still enslaved to their old natures and are therefore unable to truly keep God's commands (Romans 8:5–8).

But what about Christians for whom change seems so difficult? Scripture teaches that God sovereignly chooses to work in the lives of his people in different ways, at different times, and at different speeds. Personal revival is like corporate revival in that we cannot make it happen on our own. We are completely dependent upon God.

> Will You not Yourself revive us again,
> That Your people may rejoice in You?
> (Psalm 85:6)

As I mentioned earlier, I have had a lifelong struggle with overeating and obesity (gluttony). I have always known what I need to do to become more healthy—eat less and exercise more. I also have been aware of the spiritual issues: that I need to learn to feed on Christ rather than turning to the idol of food (Isaiah 55:1–2). Over a period of several years I made many attempts to change, but had an equal number of defeats. I felt that I had become an expert in failure. Then, a few years ago, I made another start. But this time I kept going until I had lost about fifty pounds and gained fitness to the point that I was able to run a marathon. I also enjoyed remarkable improvements in my overall health. When people would say, "Great job! What is your secret? How did you do it?" I would think of Herod, who was struck down because he did not give God the glory (Acts 12:21–23). My only reply is that God, in his mercy, sovereignly gave me grace and the discipline that I so obviously lacked for so long. He alone deserves the glory, and apart from his sustaining help, I will fail again.

God Uses Means to Accomplish Change

While we cannot change ourselves without God's sovereign mercy and help, it is good for us to apply the means that God uses to bring about change in our lives.

» *The church.* The local church is central to God's work in this age (1 Timothy 3:15), including his work of changing his people so that they are more holy and Christlike. We can expect the Lord to work in our lives as we eagerly attend worship, partake of the ordinances, hear the Bible faithfully proclaimed, and participate in the life of the body of Christ.

» *Scripture:* We should continually look to God's Word to point us both to the life-transforming gospel and to the commands and principles of wisdom. "The word of God is living and active and sharper than any two-edged sword" (Hebrews 4:12). Jesus says that as we abide in his Word, we will be fruitful (John 15:7). The psalmist pleads with God, "My soul cleaves to the dust; revive me according to Your word" (Psalm 119:25).

» *Prayer:* We should also continually pray that God will revive us and those whom we are trying to help or counsel. In Psalm 119, the psalmist repeatedly pleads with God for personal revival: "Turn away my eyes from looking at vanity, and revive me in Your ways ... Behold, I long for Your precepts; revive me through Your righteousness ... Revive me according to Your lovingkindness, so that I may keep the testimony of Your mouth ... Hear my voice according to Your lovingkindness; revive me, O LORD, according to Your ordinances" (Psalm 119:37, 40, 88, 149). Jesus offers, "Ask, and it will be given to you; seek, and you will find; knock, and it will be opened to you" (Matthew 7:7). Given the context of

Jesus' promise in the Sermon on the Mount, I think we should be asking not for earthly riches and pleasures, but that God would change us so that our lives would reflect what Jesus was teaching. Do you pray for poverty of spirit, meekness, mercy, and purity? Do you ask for a heart free from anger, lust, and deceit; for a religion which is untainted by hypocrisy; and for a life free from anxiety because you are devoted to God's kingdom? God delights to answer such prayers.

» *Trials:* God often brings circumstances into our lives which produce change that could have come no other way. The psalmist acknowledges, "Before I was afflicted I went astray, but now I keep Your word ... It is good for me that I was afflicted, that I may learn Your statutes" (Psalm 119:67, 71). James also teaches that God uses trials to bring us to maturity—that is, to change us for good: "Consider it all joy, my brethren, when you encounter various trials, knowing that the testing of your faith produces endurance. And let endurance have its perfect result, so that you may be perfect and complete, lacking in nothing" (James 1:2–4).

» *Counsel and admonition:* Sometimes we, like King David, need a Nathan to come and admonish us so that we will finally turn from sin back to the Lord (2 Samuel 12). We should thank God for those who lovingly admonish us and point us back to Christ. "And concerning you, my brethren, I myself also am convinced that you yourselves are full of goodness, filled with all knowledge and able also to admonish one another" (Romans 15:14). "Brethren, even if anyone is caught in any trespass, you who are spiritual, restore such a one in a spirit of gentleness; each one looking to yourself, so that you too will not be tempted. Bear one another's burdens, and thereby fulfill the law of Christ" (Galatians 6:1–2). "The way of a fool is right in his own eyes, but a wise man is he who listens to counsel" (Proverbs 12:15).

Ultimately, change is God's work. While we are responsible for using biblical means to pursue holiness, we are completely dependent upon the sovereign work of the Holy Spirit to give us success in his perfect timing.

Conclusion

God wants us to change and to bear fruit for his glory. "My Father is glorified by this, that you bear much fruit, and so prove to be My disciples" (John 15:8). He who began his work in us by justifying us will continue to sanctify us (Philippians 1:6).

The gospel is the key to change. As we understand our union with Christ, remember our new identity as servants of God, and find him to be our greatest delight, we are motivated and enabled to live new lives for his glory. We are also responsible for exerting effort in pursuing holiness, service, and obedience. Paul expresses how these realities work together in Philippians 2:12b–13:

> Work out your salvation with fear and
> trembling; for it is God who is at work
> in you, both to will and to work for His
> good pleasure.

The way change takes place in our lives is illustrated by Peter's experience of walking on water (Matthew 14:28–30). Just as it was completely beyond Peter's natural ability to walk on water, so it is beyond our natural ability to change for good—whether it be from lust, gluttony, materialism, substance abuse, and so on. Yet as Peter looked to Christ, he was able to walk on water. In the same way, as we continue to look by faith to Christ, we are able to do what otherwise would be impossible. And just as Peter began to sink when he took his eyes off Jesus, fearing the wind and the waves, so we will only make progress in our spiritual growth as we keep our eyes on Christ (abide in him, John 15:5). If we focus only on our efforts, we will lose sight of Jesus and his gospel, and we, like Peter, will sink.

We also have responsibility. When Jesus said, "Come!" (Matthew 14:29), Peter couldn't stay in the boat waiting for Jesus to levitate him above the water. If Peter was to walk on the water, he had to step out of the boat onto the sea. In the same way, we can't sit back in the boat merely looking at Jesus. We must hear and heed his voice to come and follow him, remembering that we will only succeed by his power. Then when we do what is humanly impossible, he will receive all the glory.

Personal Application Projects

1. Write down three areas of your life in which you are eager to change. How have unbiblical methods of change led to your failure?

2. Write out Romans 6, inserting your name where appropriate.

3. Memorize Romans 6:11.

4. Write down what you can say to yourself, when tempted, about how your union with Christ enables you to resist sin.

5. Write out Isaiah 55:1–2, inserting your area of temptation in place of "what does not satisfy."

6. Write down five practical ways in which you can learn to feed on Christ and find satisfaction in him.

7. Learn to preach the gospel to yourself every day. I recommend reading Milton Vincent's *The Gospel Primer.*[9]

8. Write down your understanding of how God's law applies to you as a Christian. Do you tend

to misuse the law, either by ignoring it or as a means of self-righteousness?

9. Go through the book of Ephesians and write down all the ways in which Paul makes practical application of gospel truths.

10. Read Psalm 119. Write out a prayer to God, asking him to revive you spiritually.

11. Write out a prayer of thanksgiving for the changes God has already accomplished in your life.

Where Can I Get More Help?

Books and Other Publications

Adams, Jay, *Growing by Grace: Sanctification and Counseling* (Stanley, NC: Timeless Texts, 2003)

Chester, Tim, *You Can Change: God's Transforming Power for Our Sinful Behaviour and Negative Emotions* (Nottingham: InterVarsity Press, 2008)

Fitzpatrick, Elyse M., and Johnson, Dennis E., *Counsel from the Cross: Connecting Broken People to the Love of Christ* (Wheaton, IL: Crossway, 2009)

Hedges, Brian, *Christ Formed in You: The Power of the Gospel for Personal Change* (Wapwallopen, PA: Shepherd Press, 2010)

Lane, Timothy S., and Tripp, Paul David, *How People Change* (Greensboro, NC: New Growth Press, 2008)

Vincent, Milton, *A Gospel Primer for Christians: Learning to See the Glories of God's Love* (Bemidji, MN: Focus Publishing, 2008)

Web Resources

The National Association of Nouthetic Counselors, www.nanc.org (for referral to biblical counselors in your area and further resources)

The Institute for Biblical Counseling and Discipleship, www.ibcd.org

END NOTES

1 All names have been changed to protect the identities of those concerned.

2 For further information on this topic see Elyse Fitzpatrick and Laura Hendrickson, *Will Medicine Stop the Pain? Finding God's Healing for Depression, Anxiety, and Other Troubling Emotions* (Chicago: Moody, 2006).

3 The great British preacher D. Martyn Lloyd-Jones declared that if our preaching doesn't produce such an objection, we aren't really preaching the gospel.

4 John R. W. Stott, *Men Made New: An Exposition of Romans 5–8* (Downers Grove, IL: InterVarsity Press, 1979), 49.

5 From D. Martyn Lloyd-Jones, *Romans: Exposition of 6:1–23: The New Man* (Grand Rapids, MI: Zondervan, 1973), 25–26.

6 John Murray, *Collected Writings*, vol. 3 (Carlisle, PA: Banner of Truth, 1982), 266–267.

7 Elyse Fitzpatrick and Dennis Johnson, Counsel from the Cross: *Connecting Broken People to the Love of Christ* (Wheaton, IL: Crossway, 2009), 123.

8 While this is the normal pattern, not every New Testament author was compelled to follow it exactly. While James founds his calls to obedience on our gospel regeneration (James 1:18), he focuses on issues of practical obedience without extensive explicit gospel

proclamation. This is probably an application of the principle of different approaches for different kinds of people (1 Thessalonians 5:14).

9 Milton Vincent, *A Gospel Primer for Christians: Learning to See the Glories of God's Love* (Bemidji, MN: Focus Publishing, 2008).

BOOKS IN THE HELP! SERIES INCLUDE...

(More titles in preparation)